Louis Le Cunff

Wonderful Brittany

Translated by Angela Moyon

ÉDITIONS OUEST-FRANCE

13 rue du Breil, Rennes

*L'aber Wrac'h near Lannilis and Plou-
guerneau (Finistère).* ▶

Top : *The Dinan Rocks in the Crozon
Peninsula.*

Middle : *a Breton cottage.*

Bottom : *Josselin Castle.*

Front cover : *Island of Groix.*

Back cover : *Notre-Dame in Châteaulin.*

WHAT BRITTANY HAS TO OFFER

An informel varied region whose population of 3,840,000 is still steeped in the Celtic tradition. 250,000 people still speak the Breton language, the last of the Celtic languages still in existence on the continent.

1,550 miles of coastline out of a total of 2,175 for France as a whole.

Some of the **westernmost headlands** in Europe - Pointe de Corsen, Pointe de Saint-Mathieu, Pointe du Toulinguet et Pointe de Pen-Hir, Pointe du Raz.

A multitude of **archipelagos and isolated islands**, among them Hoëdic, Houat, Belle-Ile, Groix, the Glénans, Sein, Molène, Ushant, Ile Vierge, Ile de Batz, Bréhat, not forgetting the islands in the Morbihan Gulf.

Gulfs, bays, natural harbours, inlets, rias, estuaries, all of them with their own outstanding beauty.

Numerous **fine sandy beaches** such as La Baule, Pornichet, Carnac, Dinard etc. and two hundred other more modest or more discreet stretches of sand.

Busy friendly towns, each of them a page of history in itself whether situated on the coast or inland - Rennes, Nantes, Brest, Lorient, Saint-Brieuc, Quimper, Saint-Malo, Dinan, Lannion, Guingamp etc.

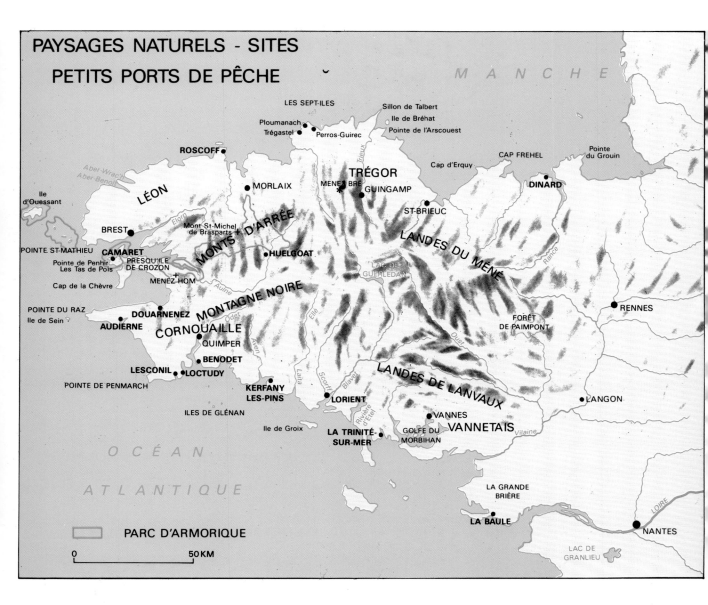

PAYSAGES NATURELS - SITES
PETITS PORTS DE PÊCHE

MANCHE

LES SEPT-ILES

Sillon de Talbert
Ile de Bréhat
Ploumanach
Trégastel ● Perros-Guirec
Pointe de l'Arscouest

ROSCOFF

CAP FREHEL
Pointe
du Grouin

Aber-Wrac'h
Aber-Benoît

TRÉGOR

Cap d'Erquy

MORLAIX
MENEZ BRÉ
GUINGAMP
DINARD

LÉON

Ile
d'Ouessant

ST-BRIEUC

Mont St-Michel
de Brasparts
MONTS D'ARRÉE

LANDES DU MÉNÉ

BREST
POINTE ST-MATHIEU
CAMARET
Pointe de Penhir
Les Tas de Pois
PRESQU'ILE
DE CROZON
HUELGOAT

Rance

LAC DE
GUERLEDAN

Cap de la Chèvre
MENEZ HOM

MONTAGNE NOIRE

FORÊT
DE PAIMPONT

RENNES

POINTE DU RAZ
Ile de Sein
DOUARNENEZ
AUDIERNE
CORNOUAILLE

QUIMPER

BENODET
LESCONIL ● LOCTUDY

POINTE DE PENMARCH

KERFANY
LES-PINS

ILES DE GLÉNAN

Ile de Groix

LORIENT

LANDES DE LANVAUX

VANNES
VANNETAIS

LANGON

LA TRINITÉ-
SUR-MER

GOLFE DU
MORBIHAN

OCÉAN

ATLANTIQUE

LA GRANDE
BRIÈRE

LA BAULE

LOIRE

NANTES

LAC DE
GRANLIEU

▭ PARC D'ARMORIQUE

0 ———————— 50 KM

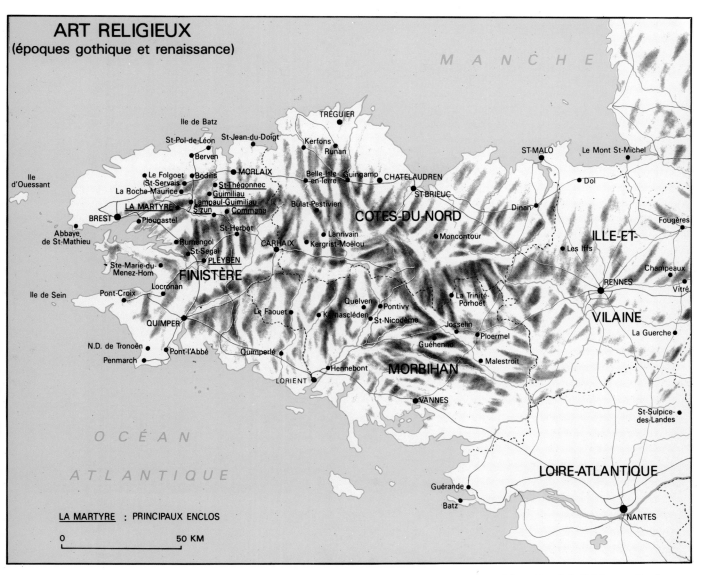

ART RELIGIEUX
(époques gothique et renaissance)

MANCHE

Ile de Batz

TRÉGUIER

St-Pol-de-Léon · St-Jean-du-Doigt
Berven
Le Folgoet · Bodilis · MORLAIX
(St-Servais · St-Thégonnec
La Roche-Maurice · Guimiliau
LA MARTYRE · Lampaul-Guimiliau
Sizun · Commana
BREST · Plougastel
St-Herbot
Abbaye · Rumengol
de St-Mathieu · St-Segal
Ste-Marie-du- · PLEYBEN
Menez-Hom
Ile de Sein · Locronan · FINISTÈRE
Pont-Croix
QUIMPER
N.D. de Tronoën · Pont-l'Abbé
Penmarch

Kerfons
Runan
Belle-Isle- · Guingamp · CHATELAUDREN
en-Terre
St-BRIEUC
Bulat-Pestivien
COTES-DU-NORD
Lanrivain · Moncontour
Kergrist-Moëlou
CARHAIX
Quelven
Le Faouet · La Trinité-
Kernascléden · Pontivy · Porhoët
St-Nicodème
Josselin
Quimperlé · Guéhenno · Ploermel
Hennebont · Malestroit
MORBIHAN
LORIENT
VANNES

Ile
d'Ouessant

ST-MALO · Le Mont St-Michel
Dol
Dinan
Fougères
ILLE-ET-
Les Iffs
Champeaux
RENNES
Vitré
VILAINE
La Guerche

St-Sulpice-
des-Landes

LOIRE-ATLANTIQUE

Guérande
Batz
NANTES

OCÉAN

ATLANTIQUE

LA MARTYRE : PRINCIPAUX ENCLOS

0 — 50 KM

Maps Patrick Mérienne, Paris.

5

Douarnenez Harbour.

Binic harbour. ▶

Small or industrial **fishing ports,** some of them among the largest on the West coast - Le Croisic, Etel, Lorient, Concarneau, Le Guilvinec, Douarnenez, Camaret, Cancale.

Shipyards (warships, merchant ships, fishing boats, pleasure craft).

Water sports centres and sailing schools all along the coast, on the islands, or even on some of Brittany's inland lakes.

The largest network of lighthouses and marker buoys anywhere in Western Europe (some of the land-based lighthouses are open to the public).

The first, and largest, tidal power station in Europe on the Rance Estuary, between Saint-Malo and Dinard.

Seabird sanctuaries, the best-known being in Sizun and on some of the islands.

The largest collections of Stone Age monuments in the world - Plouharnel, Carnac, Locmariaquer, the islands in the Morbihan Gulf and the Crozon Peninsula.

Numerous fortresses, manorhouses, aristocratic residences, and old houses.

Hundreds of **chapels, churches, wayside crosses and parish closes.**

The Château de Trécesson (Morbihan).

The remains of the ancient Brocéliande Forest *where memories of the Knights of the Round Table, Merlin the Enchanter, and Vivian the Good Fairy still linger on today.*

Very pretty **trout and salmon rivers** *(Rance, Trieux, Dossen, Elorn, Penfeld, Odet, Ellé, Scorff and Blavet, Vilaine).*

France's **top animal-producing region** *(cattle, sheep, pigs, and poultry).*

A **cattle market of European importance** *in Fougères.*

A major fruit and vegetable production area (artichokes, cauliflowers, potatoes, early vegetables, strawberries).

The largest **kaolin deposits** *in Europe used in the manufacturing of Limoges and Sarreguemines porcelain.*

Numerous **oyster farms** *(Vilaine Estuary, Morbihan Gulf, Belon area, the inlets (Abers) and Cancale).*

The first-ever **aquaculture installations** *which should make it possible in a few years' time to breed certain species of salt water fish and which should ensure the rational production of protein-rich algae.*

Probably large-scale **offshore oil fields.**

Three universities (Rennes, Nantes, Brest) and five major civilian and military academies and top-level further-education institutions.

*A **bracing climate**, full of the ozone, a revivifying area that is recommended by the medical profession (spring comes early, the summers are dry and warm, and autumn is mild).*

*Numerous **thalassotherapy centres** and seawater therapy institutions (Saint-Malo, Roscoff, Tréboul, Douarnenez, Quiberon etc.)*

*Ideal conditions for **rest and relaxation**, without destroying the biological and ecological balance.*

***Permanent contact with nature**, whether in the country or at the seaside, something that is appreciated by young and old alike.*

*An unusual **culinary and gastronomic tradition** that ranges from the simplest to the most elaborate of fare.*

***The memory of a prestigious past**, a blend of legend and history, an awareness of a certain identity, and great hopes for the future.*

***Traditional events** on a grand scale (the Cornouaille Festival in Quimper, the Blue Nets Festival in Concarneau, the Golden Broom Festival in Pont-Aven), assemblies, religious processions, ceilidhs (the ''Fest-Noz'' or evening entertainment), and pilgrimages, among them the only Islamic-Christian pilgrimage in Western Europe in memory of the seven saints of Ephesus which takes place in Vieux Marché (Côtes-du-Nord).*

*A unfathomed storehouse of **memories and artistic creation**.*

Rennes: Palais Saint-Georges and the tower of St.Melaine's Church.

THE END OF THE WORLD

A modest peninsula to the west of a continental landmass that begins on the shores of the Pacific Ocean - this is Brittany to anybody who simply looks at a globe. In this respect, it is the end of something, the "Far West" of Asia and Europe. Lying between the English Channel to the north and the Atlantic Ocean to the south, it is the last tentacular outpost of the Western world, looking out towards the setting sun.

"You see," said Saint-Pol Roux, "this is the end of the world."

For hundreds, perhaps thousands, of years millions of visitors have had the feeling that Brittany is a sort of antichamber or entrance hall to another world, a world that is both mythical and real, something perceived occasionally as other-worldly and sometimes as an empire in motion accessible to man only if he has been through an initiation process.

It is, then, easy to understand why Brittany and the neighbouring regions were described by ancient races as Armorica, **the land facing the sea.**

Today, when you say **Armorica**, most people think of Brittany, even though the Armorican Landmass extends quite far beyond the historical boundaries of the former Duchy or even beyond the boundaries of the administrative entity that has been named the Breton Development Region.

It is a fairly low-lying landmass formed for the most part by silica and clay deposits, i.e. "cold land" as the technicians put it, where the absence of limestone has led to the spread of moorland, forest and woodland.

The Pointe du Raz with the Vieille Lighthouse in the distance.

◀ *The Roc'h Trévezel near Commana.*

THE HIGHLANDS OF BRITTANY

Maps show a series of small upland ranges beyond the Rennes Basin - first of all, the **Mené** and the **Lanvaux Moors**, then further west the **Monts d'Arrée** and the **Montagne Noire** (or Black Mountain) that flank the **Chateaulin Basin**.

Don't smile when you hear the words "hills" and "mountains"! It's true that the **Highlands of Brittany** can't be compared to the Alps and the Pyrenees. Yet there is ample proof that the Armorican Landmass was once a real mountain, in the Primary Era when much of France still lay under water. And although erosion has been particularly severe over the years, it has not worn away the mountain altogether.

The ranges reach their highest altitudes in the west, but they never exceed the following rather average heights :

Tuchan Kador (Signal de Toussaines)	1,248 ft.
Montagne Saint-Michel .	1,235 ft.
Roc Trévézel	1,248 ft.
Roc Trédudon	1,206 ft.
Menez-Hom (in the Monts d'Arrée)	1,073 ft.

Modest altitudes but proud peaks all the same! You only have to see the ragged hilltops in the Arrée region to appreciate the wild pride of the upland areas of inland Brittany. From these summits, you will be able to see some outstanding scenery, panoramic views that stretch almost into infinity, encompassing bays that are unequalled anywhere in the world like Brest Harbour and Douarnenez Bay.

To the north, west and south, all the hills slope down to the sea, in steps and stairs, winding roads, and valleys crossed by sparkling rivers of silver water.

Sometimes the continent and ocean come together gently along vast stretches of fine sand or, inland, at the heads of inlets, rias, and estuaries, where the lives of whole communities are governed by the tides. But the meeting can also be brutal, competitive and tormented. There are cliffs, headlands and promontories, myriads of reefs, strings of islands, the still fragile remnants of Herculean battles that have been taking place here since the beginning of time.

The Kermorvan Peninsula near Le Conquet (Finistère).

A MILD HEALTHY CLIMATE

This basic fact governs any attempt at defining the Breton climate. And the attempt may not necessarily be successful because, in addition to the general characteristics mentioned below, you have to accept one specific idea - that there is a **multiplicity of microclimates** which, in certain gulfs, bays, or estuaries provide exceptional, stark, contrasts to the statistical averages.

For humanist geographers, and for the most rigourous climatology specialists, Brittany is a perfect example of the so-called **maritime climate**. It is damp and mild, with no great temperature differences between the coldest and hottest periods of the year.

At the Pointe Saint Mathieu, for example, there is a seasonal variation of 10°C, as against 19° in Strasburg, 16° in Bordeaux and Marseilles, and 14° in Dunkirk.

Very mild winters, and generally temperate summers - these are the basic characteristics of a climate that is widely considered as privileged because it allows the growth of subtropical plants in many places! Camelias, mimosas, and hydrangeas are a common feature in Breton gardens, providing some marvellous floral displays from mid-February onwards.

But what about the rain, you'll say ? And the wind ?

Let's look at the problem objectively.

The rain first of all. The figures prove that the rainfall is no higher in Brittany than in other regions in France that have a reputation of being drier. Here is some of the information provided by the geographer, Maurice Le Lannou, a teacher in the Collège de France :

"It rains less in Roscoff (760 mm annual rainfall) than in Bordeaux (775 mm)... Less in Rennes than in Nice (754 mm); only very slightly more in Saint-Brieuc (686 mm) than in Toulouse (623 mm)."

The truth is that **rainfall in Brittany is less continuous**. Or, to put it another way, it rains more often than elsewhere but, overall, the total rainfall is no higher. And in any case, and this will be of interest to visitors, summer in Brittany is a dry season, sometimes even too dry as far as the locals are concerned.

So you can afford to show a measure of indulgence if by any chance you come in an exceptional year.

And it has to be said that the exception may not be what you expected, since in the summer of 1976, Brittany was on several occasions the hottest and driest region in the whole of Western Europe.

So much, then, for rain and sunshine.

The Ushant-Creac'h signal station.

The Bay of the Deceased (Baie des Trépassés) between the Pointe du Raz and the Pointe du Van.

The north coast of Cape Sizun. ▶

ARMORICA'S SOUL

Now for the wind! The famous wind, Brittany's "terrible wind"! The one that comes in off the sea, the one that is capable of roaring at storm force, at hurrican strength, like a cyclone. The wind that may gust up to 95 or 120 m.p.h. The wind that strips the headlands and cliffs bare of vegetation and has literally denuded islands like Sein and Molène. You might meet this legendary wind, just as certain poets or novelists have done. But you have little chance of doing so really unless you live in Brittany for twelve months of the year, for the wind is rarely as violent as that. The storms only occur at precise periods of the year and are generally forecast in advance. Nine times out of ten, **Brittany's wind is friendly**, blowing just sufficiently to puff out the sails of the dinghies and larger sailing craft.

The wind breathes life into jibs and foresails - it is also the soul of Armorica.

The Pointe Saint-Mathieu.

BREATHE IN THE OZONE - AND LEAVE YOUR TROUBLES BEHIND

Another word in your ear - or rather, two words. The climate is **bracing** and **health-giving**. Two words and two virtues, recognised by the most eminent specialists. This is one of the few climates that can repair yearlong damage that was once considered as irreparable. It can dispel the troubles and illnesses caused in large cities or industrial centres by pollution, stress, dietary excesses, and all sorts of anxieties whether sociological, political or even metaphysical! All that thanks to the everpresent ozone in the air, the sea and the food.

Brittany's climate? A simple, basic way of recovering your health. A way that is open to everybody. That's an opinion signed **"Yours helpfully"**.

THE ARGOAT AND ARMOR

162 miles from east to west, 186 if you take in the westernmost islands in Finistère.

62 to 125 miles from north to south, or to be precise 112 miles between the Pointe du Grouin near Cancale and the Pointe de Saint-Gildas at the mouth of the Loire, 93 from the Sillon de Talbert to the furthermost headland in the Quiberon peninsula, and 62 from the Pointe de Pontusval near Brignogan to the Pointe de Penmarc'h.

These mileages calculated as the crow flies give some idea of the impressive area represented by the Breton peninsula as compared to France as a whole. In all, over 13,000 sq. miles with a population of more than 3,840,000, most of them living in the coastal belt directly affected by the sea.

With its population of 200,000, Rennes is almost the only city inland. The other large towns all lie at the head of bays, harbours, gulfs, or simply in hollows on the banks of estuaries just where the rivers meet the sea. This applies to almost all the following towns - Nantes, Vannes, Lorient, Quimper, Concarneau, Douarnenez, Brest, Morlaix, Saint-Brieuc, and Saint-Malo.

And so, from the very first moment, visitors will see the twin facets of the specific identity of Brittany and the Bretons - the **Argoat**, the woodland or forest region, and the **Armor**, the country of the sea. On one side, there is almost total sedentarity, with a rural population; on the other, along a narrow coastal strip, a permanent communion with the wide open spaces of the ocean.

The development of road and rail links over the past fifty years has caused relative unification in life styles. Yet as far as sensitivity and traditions are concerned, there are still very real differences between coastal Bretons and the inland communities. This is a fact that should not be ignored. It gives visitors a closer understanding of **the Bretons** who gave the Armorican peninsula its name.

The Huelgoat Forest.

Rennes. Right : *Place du Palais.* Left, top : *the Champ-Jacquet.* Centre : *the theatre on the Place de la Mairie.* ▶

21

ARMORICA AND THE ARMORICANS

To start with, you have to remember that the Bretons were the last to arrive in this region where successions of very different peoples settled over tens of thousands of years.

Along the present coastline, experts have found traces of settlements dating back to the Early Bronze Age. The siting of the settlements and the remains that were unearthed there would seem to suggest that the men and women of the oldest period in Armorican prehistory were already relying on the sea for most of their food and livelihood. But variations in the coastline caused by a rise in sea level or the sinking of the continental landmass have submerged most of the remains left by the first human settlements. Digs undertaken in Guiriden in the Glénan archipelago uncovered a tall skeleton. Unfortunately it was not complete but it proves the existence of men who were more than 6 ft. 6 ins. tall. Elsewhere, for example in the tiny island of Téviec near Quiberon, graves were found containing male skeletons with a height ranging from only 4 ft. 10ins. to 5 ft. 3 ins.

Giants and dwarfs! Just like characters from the Armorican legend... As if popular memory had come together with prehistoric reality!

◄ *Glomel standing stone (Côtes-du-Nord).*

Gavrinis tumulus : the engravings are six thousand years old! ►

Ile aux Moines in the Morbihan Gulf.

MINOS, CADIZ, AND THE MORBIHAN !

The next people to settle here erected the standing stones. Physically, they must have resembled the Ligurians. They lived along the coast and were a seafaring people who, long before the dawn of history, had their own kind of civilisation.

Bronze, iron, tin, the Islands of Tin - we have now entered a truly fabulous world ! Several thousands of years before Armorica became a Celtic land, techniques had been developed in the peninsula at the tip of Europe that implied extensive knowledge of astronomy and mechanics. And apparently it was the Morbihan coast which was the most active in this respect. Camille Jullian describes it as follows :

"The men of the Morbihan were the masters of the Western seas. They played the same role, no doubt at the same time, as the people of Cadiz at the gateway to the Great Strait, and as the men of Crete in the Eastern Mediterranean. There was a continuous link between all these leaders of a sea-based society. Minos, Cadiz, and the Morbihan - the unbroken original trade route, taken by boats, merchandise, and the civilisation of Antiquity.."

The Roche-aux-Fées (Little People Rock). ▶

The passage grave at Le Mougau-Vian near Commana.

BRITTANY OF
THE STANDING STONES

There are still many traces of this far-distant period throughout the peninsula. And today, Brittany offers Prehistory enthusiasts larger concentrations of megaliths than any other region in the world - **menhirs** (long standing stones), **dolmens** (stone tables), **tumuli and passage graves, peulvens, cromlechs** (stone circles) etc.

Carnac (Morbihan) is an impressive spectacle and we can only regret the irreparable damage done over the centuries to the prehistoric sites in **Menec, Kermario** and **Kerlescan**. As they stand today, these three groups of alignments are a fantastic sight

and an incitement to meditation. In all, there are almost 3,000 standing stones, the remains of a veritable forest of megaliths which, according to the experts, once formed a sort of solar calendar.

Not far from Carnac, on the road from Plouharnel to Erdeven and Etel, are the **Kerzhero alignments**, where one thousand stones cover a distance of more than a mile. Some of the stones are more than 16 ft. high.

In the Crozon Peninsula (Finistère), the **Lagat-Jar alignments** comprise some 140 standing stones.

Throughout the peninsula, there

are isolated menhirs and dolmens (Champ Dolent near Dol, Locmariaquer, Saint-Pierre-Quiberon, island of Er Lannic in the Morbihan Gulf), and passage graves and tumuli e.g. in the island of Gavrinis, in the Rhuys Peninsula, at Commana, at La Roche aux Fées etc.

In many places, the menhirs have a cross engraved in the stone itself. But this Christianisation of the stones took place much later, almost certainly after the arrival of the Breton immigrants.

The alignments in Carnac. ▶

The Barnenez cairn (Finistère).

The great Larcuste Stone Age cairn in Colpo (Morbihan).

THE GRANDEUR AND DECLINE OF THE CELTS OF ARMORICA

In the meantime, i.e. from the period that saw the setting up of the menhirs and dolmens until the arrival of the Bretons, a population of Celts had already settled in the peninsula and had consolidated, if not developed, the brilliant civilisation based on maritime trade described by Jullian in conjunction with the indigenous people.

Organised firstly in tribes and gradually in settlements, this civilisation consisted of the following peoples : the **Redoni** in the region of Redon and Rennes ; the **Curiosolites** beyond the R.Rance around present-day Corseul ; the **Osmismens** in the western Finistère ; the **Namneti** on both banks of the R.Loire ; and finally, on the shores of the Morbihan Gulf and along to the boundaries of the Osmismens' territory, there were the **Veneti** who seemed to have been the masters of the tin trade for several centuries. And so it was until the Roman conquest.

"**The Veneti,**" wrote Caesar, "**constitute far and away the most powerful people along the coast...They far surpass the other peoples because of their scientific knowledge and experience in navigation.**"

It was this people who set up the strongest resistance to occupation by the Roman troops. In 52 B.C. Caesar had to intervene personally and launch the Roman fleet against the mighty ships of the Veneti. The battle took place somewhere between Belle-Ile, the Quiberon Peninsula, and the Morbihan Gulf. It ended in the defeat of the Veneti. And the rest needs no retelling. "**In order to teach the Barbarians greater respect for the rights of the ambassadors in the future, Caesar decided to deal a severe blow. He had the entire Senate executed and auctioned off the remainder.**"

Mercury, a Roman God. A bronze statuette. Brittany Museum (Rennes).

Belle-Ile. ▶

33

The Croisic Peninsula.

◄Belle-Ile.

Erquy Harbour. ►

36

Houat.

Hoëdic.

Brittany as seen by Mathurin Méheut : Getting ready for the procession to Our-Lady-of-Joy.

THE ARRIVAL
OF THE BRETONS

So ended the epic story of the Veneti of Morbihan... The entire population of Armorica was now subjected to the famous **Pax romana**, or Roman peace ! A peace that was to last several hundred years, until the Germanic tribes began to put pressure on the British Isles and on the continental part of the Roman Empire, thereby setting off one of the greatest periods of major change in the history of Europe.

The Angles, Jutes, and Saxons landed in the island of Britain and pushed the Britons westwards. Many of them crossed the Channel and landed on the western shores of Europe, mainly in Armorica.

And how did the Gallo-Roman population receive the newcomers in these regions ? There is only very fragmented information on this subject but one thing is sure - in less than two hundred years, the Bretons imposed their language, customs, and social structure throughout the peninsula. Armorica became so Britonised than it became known as **Little Britain** (Petite Bretagne), soon to be changed to **Brittany**.

This is a period about which we have little concrete knowledge, a period in which Christian and Celtic wonders are given greater importance than History. Yet the collective Breton subconscious has continued to feed on this very period over the course of the centuries. Most of the place names and surnames date from this fabulous time. It was this period, too, that has provided the most prestigious episodes in Breton legends, in particular the stories surrounding the founding of Brittany's first bishoprics and the legends of the towns that disappeared beneath the waves (Is, Tolente, Occismor, Lexobie, and Les Birvideaux).

Concarneau.

The Pointe du Pen-Hir.

The radome in Pleumeur-Bodou.

Father Trébeurden on the Pink Granite Coast. ▶

PLOU, KER AND TRE IN ABUNDANCE

Even visitors who are not place-name experts cannot but be struck by the large number of places beginning with **Plou, Plo, Pleu, Plé, Ploe,** or **Plu,** all of them equivalent to, or derived from, the Latin "plebs". Names like Ploufragan, Plougastel, Ploumiliau, Ploumanach, and Ploemeur, Pleumeur, Ploemel, Ploërmel, Plozevet, Plumiliau, Pluzunet, Plélan, Pleyben etc. In all, after fifteen centuries, more than one hundred and thirty parishes have kept alive through their names the memory of the very first Breton communities. They settled in Armorica with their bishops, who were often honoured as saints (as they still are today).

As an example, let's take a look at the meaning of some of the place names :

Ploërdut : the parish of St. Ildut
Ploërmel : the monk's parish
Plescop : the bishop's parish
Ploemeur and Pleumeur : the large parish

Less common are the **Tré**, which come from the ancient "**trebo**". They were probably subdivisions of the **parishes**: Trébeurden, Tréhorenteuc, Tréméven, Tréguier. Also less frequent are the **lan** which often indicate a hermitage or a small monastery e.g. Lampaul, Landerneau, Landivisiau, Lannilis, Lannion, Lanrivoaré, Lanvollon etc.

Another series of place-names includes the root **Ker**, which comes from the old Breton words **caër** or **cazr**, which themselves come directly from the Latin **castrum** or its Celtic equivalent. So we have names like Kernascléden, Kerlouan, Kerroc'h, Kermario, Kérity, Kergrist, Kergonan, Kerfeunteun, as well as a few names beginning with Car such as Carhaix.

Pleyben Church.

◀ *Tréguier : the Romanesque cathedral and Gothic cloisters.*

THE BRITTANY
OF THE SAINTS

If you list all the place names beginning with **plou, tré, lan,** or **ker,** you will have at least half, if not more, of all the places in Brittany. To end with, you might like to add all the names of saints which have come down from the ancient Celtic stories of their lives. They tell of very colourful characters who were both monks and warriors, some of them hermits, but all of them very close to their people - Brieuc, Malo, Gildas, Caradec, Enogat, Herbot, Diboan, Gwénolé, Ké or Quay. Not forgetting Riec (or Riou), Ronan, and Sezny, whose memories linger on in Lanriec and Riec-sur-Belon, in Saint-Renan and Locronan, and in Guissény (the **guic**, or village, of St. Sezny).

During their lifetime or in the couple of hundred years following their death, some of these venerable personages enjoyed a quite outstanding amount of influence and today they are still the patron saints of Brittany's ancient bishoprics - **Patern** in Vannes, **Corentin** in Quimper, **Paul-Aurélien** in St-Pol-de-Léon, **Tugdual** in Tréguier, **Brioc** in Saint-Brieuc, **Malo** in Aleth Saint-Malo, and **Samson** in Dol. The Middle Ages fervently added the name of Yves Hélory to this list; he was the famous St. Yves of Tréguier.

45

St. Gwénolé. Landévennec.

St. Yves' tomb (19th century). Tréguier Cathedral. ▶

Locronan has been the setting of many a film. This is a scene from "Les Chouans" directed by Philippe de Broca (1987).

◄*Traditional Bigouden head-dresses, shown here during a religious procession.*

Pontivy Castle (Morbihan).

THE BRETONS ENTER THE HISTORY BOOKS

Once this mythical period was past, i.e. during the Carolingian period elsewhere in Europe, there were already the stirrings of a Breton state, and the outstanding figure of the times was undoubtedly Duke Noménoë.

He was a strange character who, as was usual in the politics of the day, was totally unscrupulous. He began by putting down the uprisings that had broken out in the Vannes region (then known as **Broërec**), acting on behalf of Louis the Pious, Charlemagne's son and heir. After that, he turned against Louis the Pious' successors, i.e. Lothar and Charles the Bald, and became the implacable enemy of the Franks. So it was that, in 845 A.D., he inflicted a crushing defeat on Charles the Bald in Ballon, north of Redon, captured Rennes and Nantes, and led the Breton troops into the Touraine.

It has also been said that Noménoë was crowned King of Brittany in Dol. Is this true? It is difficult to find any historical evidence but what is certain is that he governed Brittany like a true sovereign, eliminating all the Frankish bishops in Brittany with the help of St. Conwoïon.

The Duchesne Tower in the Rue Nantaise (Rennes). ▶

His son, **Erispoë** (851-857) continued his father's work, again defea-
ting the Franks in Angers and gaining recognition for himself as King
of Brittany, this time an undisputed
fact. From then on, the kingdom
consisted of the Rennes and Nantes
regions and stretched south of the
Loire to the Retz area.

This is the first appearance of
what we might call **Historical Brittany**. A Brittany which was to last
for six hundred years, with alterna-
ting periods of tragedy and
grandeur.

One of the tragic periods was the
one which, in the 10th century, saw
the great invasions by the Viking
pirates. The Breton abbeys and their
treasures were choice morsels for the
Norsemen, who ransacked the
abbeys in Landévennec, Redon, and
Plélan as well as the cathedrals in
Nantes and Vannes.

One of the Breton chiefs, Alain
Barbetorte, who had sought refuge
at the English Court, landed in Dol
with a number of troops and attemp-
ted, with almost immediate success,
to boot the Viking invaders out of
Brittany. He settled in Nantes and
acquired the title of Duke of Brittany. Soon the entire country was
integrated into the feudal system that
was gradually spreading throughout
Europe.

FOUR CENTURIES OF WAR

Over the centuries, the feudal history of Brittany has been the subject
of hundreds of books. All of them
emphasise the covetousness which,
until the early 16th century, made
Brittany a pawn and a jousting
ground in the game that opposed
France and England. For four hundred years, directly or through partisans acting as intermediaries, the
two major powers of the day enga-
ged in merciless combat in the
peninsula.

Combourg Castle.

52

This is not the place to mention more than a few of the dates that mark this exceedingly long period :

1133 : Treaty of Gisors. Louis VI the Fat, King of France, recognised the sovereignty of the Dukes of Normandy (by then Kings of England) over the Counts of Brittany.

1148 - 1203 : sovereignty of the Plantagenets of England over Brittany.

1203 : Death of Count Geoffrey of Brittany. His son, Arthur, was murdered by his uncle John Lackland. The Breton estates fell into the hands of Arthur's half-sister, Princess Alix, who was soon married to Peter of Dreux, Louis the Fat's great-grandson. Brittany passed to the Capets and the Breton princes rendered homage directly to the King of France. But it was **simple homage** ; the King was not their **liege lord**.

1237 - 1250 : Peter of Dreux, generally known as Pierre Mauclerc or Count Perron, held very real power and quickly turned against the Kings of France, firstly against Philip Augustus and the Regent Blanche of Castille, then against King Louis (later St.Louis) himself. Again the Count of Brittany paid homage to the King of England.

1250 - 1341 : The Counts of Brittany considered themselves as vassals of the King of France. For several years, one of them, John II (1286 - 1305) again turned to England, but he was later reconciled with the King of France, Philip the Fair, who raised Brittany to a dukedom as a reward.

Josselin Castle.

La Bretêche Castle (Loire-Atlantique).

▲ *Josselin : the Neo-Gothic dining room.*

◄ *Josselin : the Rue des Vierges.*

THE HOUSE OF BRITTANY

Pierre de Dreux, dit Mauclerc (1213-1237)
Husband of Alix sister of Duke Arthur of Brittany, murdered by Jean Lackland
Became DUKE on Alix' death and abdicated in 1237

Jean I, Duke of Brittany (1237-1286)

Jean II, Duke of Brittany (1286-1305)

Arthur II, Duke of Brittany (1305-1312)
married twice :

in 1275, Marie, Vicountess of Limoges

Jean III,
"the Good"
(1312-1341)
Duke of
Brittany
died
heirless

Guy de Penthièvre

Jeanne
de Penthièvre,
wife of
Charles Blois,
killed
at the Battle
of Auray
en 1364

Pierre

in 1291, Yolande de Dreux

Jean IV
de Montfort
(1364-1399)
Duke
of Brittany
husband
of Jeanne
of Flandre

Jeanne

Béatrice

Alix

Jean IV, Duke of Brittany
(1364-1399)

Jean V, Duke of Brittany
(1399-1442)

François I, Duke of Brittany
(1442-1450)

Pierre II, Duke of Brittany
(1450-1457)

François II, Duke of Brittany
(1458-1488)

Anne of Brittany (1488-1514),
Duchess of Brittany
married successively :

in 1490,
Maximilien
of Habsbourg

in 1491,
Charles VIII,
King of France
died
heirless

in 1499,
Louis XII,
King of France

Claude France
1514 m.
François d'Angoulême
(future François I) ;
inherited the duchy
on death
of Anne of Brittany

François,
Crown Prince of France
in 1532, François I
succeded in gaining
acceptance for the Act
of Union linking
Brittany and France

The castle in Nantes.

Nantes : the castle of the Dukes of Brittany.

Les Rochers, near Vitré.

BLOIS v. MONTFORT
or THE WAR OF
BRETON SUCCESSION

1341 - 1365 : Duke John III died without leaving a direct heir and two of his brothers' children !aid claim to the Duchy - Jeanne de Penthièvre, wife of Charles of Blois (who was himself the nephew of the King of France, Philip VI of Valois) and John of Montfort who was allied to the King of England. This was the start of the **War of Breton Succession**, which was in fact part of the One Hundred Years' War. In all, the duchy suffered twenty-four years of fighting, murder, pillaging, and misery. But one figure stood out above the others - Duguesclin, who was a staunch supporter of the French camp and who, because of

this, found himself obliged to fight his own compatriots, most of them supporters of Montfort.

The Penthièvres were defeated, firstly in La Roche-Derrien in 1347 (i.e. a year after the Battle of Crecy), and again in Auray where Charles of Blois, Jeanne de Penthièvre's husband, was killed. The Montforts took charge of Brittany's affairs.

Although the first representative of this family, John IV, had been brought up at the English Court, he would no doubt have confirmed his loyalty to King Charles VI of France if the monarch had not committed the fatal error of proclaiming the annexation of the Duchy. Brittany

again found itself in the English camp, with the exception of a small number of noblemen such as Olivier de Clisson, later Constable of France.

1399 : John VI succeeded his father and, until 1442, he made every effort to keep his Duchy out of the bloody confrontation between France and England. This was a happy period in the Duchy's history, and a period of expansion for seaports such as Bourgneuf, Nantes, Le Croisic, Douarnenez, Morlaix, Saint-Malo etc. It was a major period of construction, too, when Brittany acquired large numbers of castles, churches, and chapels.

La Chapelle-Chaussée (Ille-et-Vilaine) : 16th-century castle.

THE "INSANE WAR"
Saint-Aubin-du-Cormier

In 1484, Duke François II of Brittany, who had no male heir, began negotiations with Anne of Beaujeu, then Regent of France, to ensure that his daughters' rights to the succession would be recognised, having already received the approval of the States of Brittany.

His eldest daughter was called Anne, later to become the famous Duchess Anne. The five hundredth anniversary of her birth was celebrated in 1977.

This did not prevent François II from allying himself with a few of the great noblemen at the Court of France who were plotting against the Regent. Among them was the Duke of Orleans, later King Louis XII of France. This marked the outbreak of the "Insane War" that was to last for four years.

La Bourbansais Castle.

Suscinio Castle in the Rhuys Peninsula.

Châteaugiron Castle.

Saint-Malo : the National Fort.

◀ *Saint-Malo : Duchess Anne's House.*

On 28th July 1488, the Breton troops led by the Duke of Orleans were defeated by the Duke de la Trémoïlle in Saint-Aubin-du-Cormier, not far from Fougères. On the famous **Lande de la Rencontre** (Battle Moor) 6,000 Bretons were massacred. Their leaders, who were invited to dine with the Duke de la Trémoïlle, were treacherously murdered. The only two to be spared were the Duke of Orleans and the Prince of Orange. After this, Duke François II of Brittany was required to sign a treaty stipulating that he could not marry his daughters without the consent of the King of France. Four of Brittany's fortresses were held as security (Saint Aubin, Fougères, Saint Malo, and Dinan) and were occupied by La Trémoïlle's troops. Duke François passed away a few weeks later, a broken man.

And this is how the little Duchess Anne, then aged only twelve, first walked onto the History's stage.

Around her, the supporters of independence stood firm against the partisans of the King of France led by one Rohan. England, Austria, and the Kingdom of Aragon all sent reinforcements into Brittany, while La Trémoïlle and his allies continued to defend the King's interests locally.

Once again, Brittany was overrun by footsoldiers and brigands. Peasants' revolts became rife. Soon La Trémoïlle controlled the whole of Brittany, except for Rennes and **the little girl living in the town.**

Saint-Malo : the ramparts and harbour.

Saint-Malo en l'Ile. ▶

The Rue de Dinan in Saint-Malo.

Saint-Malo : the town hall. ▶

Dinan and the Rance Valley.

◄*Dinan : Old Mother Pourcel's House (late 15th - 16th centuries).*

DUCHESS AND QUEEN

On 19th December 1490, Anne of Brittany married Emperor Maximilian of Austria by proxy. But her entourage did their utmost to prove to her that the marriage was null and void. From then on, the little Duchess had only one choice - she had to play an active role in politics, and she threw herself into it wholeheartedly. It was a choice that was to take a child of fourteen quite naturally to the throne of France. In order to save her Duchy, she agreed to marry the young King Charles VIII.

The wedding took place on 6th December 1491 in the castle at Langeais - and Anne of Britanny became Queen of France. The marriage contract stipulated that, if the King died childless, Anne would have to marry the heir to the throne.

This is what happened just over six years later. On 8th April 1498, Charles VIII died as the result of an accident. However obstinately she defended her title of Duchess of Brittany, Anne may also have been pleased to remain Queen of France, for the position enabled her to settle old scores with former enemies, in particular those who had entered the King's service. On 8th January 1499, she married the new monarch, Louis XII, i.e. the Duke of Orleans, the former rebel who had led the Breton troops in Saint-Aubin-du-Cormier.

Again, the contract stipulated that Brittany would maintain its traditional rights and privileges. It was indicated in particular that the title of Duke of Brittany could not be granted to the heir to the crown of France.

Dinan Castle (late 14th century) : Duchess Anne's keep.

4th AUGUST 1532 :
THE ACT OF UNION

Yet Anne of Brittany, the woman described by the writer Brantôme as **wise, honest, speaking well of her fellows, very kind and of a subtle turn of mind,** the political brain with the indomitable spirit, forgot to make official the one thing closest to her heart - the prohibiting of marriage between the heir to the throne of France and any future Duchess of Brittany.

This was the point of convergence that Destiny (or History) were to choose ; Louis XII and Anne of Brittany did have one son, but he did not live for long. The other children by their marriage were girls - Claude and Renée.

So, yet again the Duchy was to be governed by a woman. On the French side, the legitimate heir to the throne was Louis XII's cousin, Duke François of Angoulême. To the very end of her days, Queen Anne was to make every attempt to prevent the marriage of the future king and the future duchess while Louis XII, on the contrary, did everything possible to promote it.

As for the States General of Brittany, they were also agreeable to the marriage. They soon received the backing of the members of the Breton Parliament. Yet nothing could wear down the Queen's resistance and it was not until one year after her death, i.e. in 1515, that the wedding took place.

For the second time in history, the event had two simultaneous results - a Duchess of Brittany became Queen of France. And how apparently fragile was the last legal barrier to the merging of royal and ducal crowns.

It was for this reason, which François I considered as inevitable, that he encouraged the States of Brittany to adopt the famous **Act of Union,** by which Queen Claude would bequeath the Duchy of Brittany to her husband in perpetuity.

This occurred on 4th August 1532. A historic date if ever there was...

Dinan : the Clock Tower (late 15th century).

From then on, the official history of Brittany would be part of the history of France itself. Yet, over the following centuries, there were a number of hiccups that were interpreted as the resurgence of the Breton will to be different. Such were a number of events dating from the Wars of the League at the end of the 16th century, when the Duke of Mercoeur was suspected of harbouring secret hopes of reviving the Duchy of Brittany, for his own benefit.

In the same way, during the peasants' revolts in 1695, the famous "Red Bonnets" led by the solicitor Le Balp claimed rights based on "Armorican liberties". The terrible repression that followed this outbreak of civil disorder is well known through the letters written by Madame de Sévigné.

During the Regency, the Pontcallec Conspiracy could also be seen as the survival, among a small portion of the aristocracy, of a certain Breton desire to redeem lost territory. The most important of all, though, was the Chouans', or Royalist, Revolt which was so very different to all the other battles that took place during the war in Vendée. Here again, there were those who believed that, somewhere among the Breton Chouans' deepest convictions, there was a more or less conscious wish to restore ancient privileges to Brittany.

The list is endless..But with the passing years, this real or imaginary territorial desire has changed. Although there are now times when the "Breton problem" or "Brittany's future" have to be discussed, it most frequently occurs when central government is deemed to be too excessive. It is then essential, in order to shed light on the region's specific characteristics and the particular characteristics of a population that is simply not like others.

THE LEAGUE, REVOLTS, AND CONSPIRACIES

It's true that the Bretons were granted a certain number of important rights, freedoms and privileges, but with the signing of the **Act of Union**, a new page of History had been turned.

73

The town walls in Vannes.

▲*Vannes : the Place Saint-Pierre.*

◄*Vannes : the wash-houses on the banks of the R. Marle. They date from the 17th and 18th centuries.*

The "Bélèm" in Saint-Malo.

CELTS TO THE FORE

Whatever the case, the Bretons have expressed themselves within France as a whole throughout the last four hundred years and it has to be said that they have often done so with great success.

In many fields, Bretons have had pride of place.

It's natural to think immediately of the kings of the sea, the explorers of new lands like Coatanlem and Porsmoguer (better known as Pri-

mauguet), Jacques Cartier, Jacques Cassard, Duguay-Trouin, Kerguélen, Bouvet, Marion-Dufresne, Mahé de la Bourdonnaye, Huon de Kermadec, Surcouf etc. And there have been illustrious men of medecine such as Laënnec, Broussais, and Alphonse Guérin. Not forgetting scientists and inventers such as Maupertuis, Protet, Dupuy de Lôme etc.

But more importantly, it has been in the realm of philosophy and literary creation that the influence of Brittany's sons has been felt most over the course of the centuries, with men like Chateaubriand, Lamennais, Renan, Tristan Corbière and their present-day successors Guéhenno, Louis Guilloux, and Pierre-Jakez Hélias. None of this would probably have been possible without the intense fermentation of the Celtic civilisation, even if it was covered by a thin layer of Latin culture.

Things began far back in time, when the arts and technology were not yet the preserve of the best-educated classes and creativity was based on popular inspiration.

Whether Armorican or Breton, the Western peninsula has always been the land of bards. Without necessarily wishing to uphold the opinions of La Villemarqué who believed that the oral tradition had retained texts dating back to the days of the Ancient Gauls, it is generally thought that the poetry of the bards survived in all the Celtic countries long after the Roman conquest and the arrival of Christianity. It is also known with a greater degree of certainty that, between the 10th and 11th centuries, Breton minstrels and storytellers were famous throughout Europe.

And there were many such minstrels, harpists, and jugglers accompanying the Breton barons when, with William the Conqueror, they set off to defeat England in 1066. Their names have not come down to us today but their memory lives on. Throughout the century that followed the replacement of the Anglo-Saxons by the Normans, Brittany's poets enjoyed a privileged position at the English court.

The reason for this was that the Breton poets were unrivalled in Europe for their ''lays'', or songs. Many of the events and feelings of these faroff days are still known to us because of their poetry, which they sang to the accompaniment of some quite inspired harp-playing.

Saint-Malo : statue of Surcouf.

Li ancient Bretun curteis
Firent le lai pour remembrer
Que hum nel deust pas oublier

The Ancient Bretons, versed in
    courtly ways,
Created the lay to remind us
Of that which we must not forget.

Courtliness, love, justice, glory, the spirit of chivalry, faithfulness to God - Brittany's minstrels knew how to express it all. This is why they were brought from deep in the heart of their peninsula to entertain the most sumptuous courts.

And thus it was for several centuries. It would be no exaggeration to say that Brittany's harpists, like their cousins over the Channel, played a very large part in popularising the **theme of Brittany** which was considered in its day to be the equal of the **themes of France and Rome-the-Great.**

Saint-Guénolé rocks near Penmarc'h.

Menez-Kador in the Crozon Peninsula. ▶

King Arthur may have been a mythical figure or a historical hero and the Knights of the Round Table may have made Tintagel in Cornwall the centre of their universe. That did not stop the quest for the Holy Grail continuing along the pathways and through the forests of Brittany, where Merlin the Enchanter and Vivian the Good Fairy also lived.

It was at this fabulous time that the magical powers of the **love potion** came into existence. Once it has been drunk, even by mistake, it will arouse the one thing that is more inflammable that all the oil in Arabia and more explosive than a charge of TNT. Ten centuries later, the radioactive fallout from these mysterious explosions is still raining down on the world, explosions that, since Tristan and Isolde's ship, have shaken the sensitivity of the Western world.

Chateaubriand by Girodet (1807). Saint-Malo Museum.

CHATEAUBRIAND AND THE ROMANTIC REVIVAL

In the 19th century, there was yet another explosion - the Romantic Revival!

The cause of this new European earthquake was a young Breton named Chateaubriand. He was born in Saint-Malo in 1768 and, as a youth, he lived with his family in Combourg. A unique destiny awaited him!

His favourite season was autumn, when the reeds began to rustle and the wind began to stir up the first dead leaves. Between the young man and Mother Nature all around him, there gradually developed a sort of secret relationship. He listened to the great mysterious voices that soughed in the marshes and woodlands. In his unquiet soul, an unknown malady was beginning to stir - melancholy.

"It was in Combourg," he said, "that I became what I am now, there that I began to feel the first attack of this melancholy that has stalked me throughout my life, this sadness that has been my torment and my joy."

This is how Chateaubriand, the man from Brittany, gave birth to the myth of the melancholy Breton, among others. After him, generations of Breton poets, novelists, and philosophers convinced themselves that they belonged to a race that was intrinsically sad. Even the great Renan was taken in, stating in his "Prayer on the Acropolis":

"I was born, blue-eyed goddess, of barbarian parents, among the good virtuous Cimmerians who live on the shores of a dark sea bristling

80

with rocks, constantly battered by storms. The sun is almost unknown... Clouds look colourless and even joy itself is tinged with sadness.''

The magic of language, the inebriation of words, the wildness of the imagination... There is all that in Chateaubriand, Renan and many of their successors.

But this is not the only mood of Breton creativity. From Noël du Fail in the 16th century to Yves-Marie Rudel and P-J Hélias, not forgetting Le Guyader, Breton writers have been breathing comedy and truculence all over us - not that this precludes a deep-seated sensitivity.

In fact, the Breton soul, like Brittany itself, cannot be systematically dissected for it has countless components and innumerable examples. If you dream of harmony and oneness, then this is not the place for you. Here, everything is multifaceted, contradictory, and difficult to identify.

And yet...

THE BRETON CHARACTER

The scenery and people have secret affinities which thousands of years of mutual love have engraved in the earth, sky and hearts of the region. The storms and tempests do not only unleash the waves of the ocean; they swell souls and form character. Even the mist is not content with simply casting its woolly mantle over the headlands and islands of the end of the world; it occasionally creates a

Port-Tudy on the island of Groix.

A traditional house on the Ile aux Moines.

dusk-like softness in the very depths of a being, something that inspires meditation. But just as a shaft of sunlight soon returns the rugged outlines to the coast, so the hearts of the people soon overcome their melancholy, and the Bretons know better than any other race how to ensure that the most daring projects become reality. Fashioned by difficult circumstances, spurred on by a need to fight, the men of Armorica have no hesitation in launching into the defence of lost causes merely because it is a fine gesture. But if, by any chance, their efforts are rewarded by victory, they usually remain modest in their hour of triumph.

Are they taciturn or dour? No, that is not really the correct way of describing the Breton character. It is true that the people can wile away many a long hour without showing any need to communicate their deepest feelings. But the silence is never final. As soon as their attention is taken by some forceful idea, they immediately become talkative, enthusiastic, passionate, sometimes even refusing to listen to the other side of the argument.

Their courage, though, is in no doubt; one might even call them foolhardy. Only one thing frightens them. Death? Certainly not. It accompanies the Breton people every

minute of the day. No, it is simply a fear of looking ridiculous. It is this fear of being laughed at that often explains why they are so introverted. When only a short step away from success, give them one ironic smile and they may lose some of their self-assurance. This is no doubt the cause of the pride, reserve, and shyness that often serve only to mask an innate timidity.

A mill on the R. Vilaine. ▲

The Moulin du Boël (17th century mill) near Rennes. ▶

MAKING REAL CONTACT

This, then, is the people living in an area stretching from the rivers Loire and Couesnon out to the furthest-flung headlands of the European continent. In some places, it is some particular facet of their character that is more pronounced; elsewhere, another characteristic will be in greater evidence. But the Gallo speakers of eastern Brittany and the Breton speakers of the west accept each other as brothers and there is no question of setting one against the other in some artificially-established classification. Both of them feel the same deep-seated fervour. Their hopes and aspirations overlap, complement each other, and are often easily identifiable. Over the centuries, all this has created an outstanding popular epic.

This is why you have to know how to make contact with this quite unique world.

For visitors arriving from the east, some of the towns in Ille-et-Vilaine and Loire-Atlantique can be seen as the **gateways to the region**. Among them are Fougères, Vitré, La Guerche-de-Bretagne, Chateaubriant, Ancenis, Clisson and Machecoul.

From north to south-east on the marches of Brittany, there are ruins of the old fortresses that once provided the Duchy's defence, many of them still majestic. From first glance at these impressive buildings, or at least at the ones which have withstood the ravages of time or warfare, it is obvious that the Barons along the marches of Brittany were by no means noblemen of little importance!

FOUGÈRES

The first fortress in Fougères was built in the 11th century but the castle that is seen today was built between the 11th and 15th centuries.

Fougères Castle.

La-Guerche-de-Bretagne.

The group of buildings overlooking the R.Nançon covers more than one-and-a-half hectares and has thirteen towers with names that are often highly evocative - Mélusine Tower, Papegaut (or Popinjay) Tower, La Trémoille Tower etc. From legend to history ! And on to literature since some of the events in Balzac's novel, "Les Chouans", were set against the background of Fougères Castle.

Nowadays, Fougères is one of Ille-et-Vilaine's sub-prefectures, with a population of just 22,000. Its main industry is shoe-making, and it has the largest meat market any where in Europe.

LA GUERCHE-DE-BRETAGNE

The fortress was razed to the ground in 1739. But the town still has a number of old houses.

La Guerche-de-Bretagne, which lies 14 miles to the south of Vitré on the marches of Brittany, has something of the Anjou and Loire Valley about it. It has spread over a pleasant tranquil spot at low altitude, a docile setting for a town. A **Matz,** a plain wooden keep surrounded by several rows of stakes, was originally built on the feudal motte, an artificial hill that was already in existence in those faroff days. It stood in a marshy depression to the east of the Rue de la Chartre. In the 15th century, this wooden keep was replaced by a stone keep surrounded by quartz granite ramparts - the "Castle" razed to the ground in 1739. Around it grew up a small feudal village called La Guerche. Although, until the French Revolution, it was part of the parish of Rannée, it was also the seat of a large estate.

The lords of La Guerche had the privilege of carrying the Bishop of Rennes' throne when he first entered the cathedral - a privilege they shared with the lords of Châteaugiron, Vitré and Aubigné. La Guerche was a noble estate, described as a barony, which enjoyed the right to dispense Justice and covered eight parishes. It also had a "Municipal Community", the forerunner of today's Town Council, and was one of the forty-two towns in Brittany with the right to send representatives to the Provincial Estates.

In their heyday, c. 1245, the Knights Templar founded one of only four commanderies in Brittany in La Guerche and it had an abundance of possessions. In order to ensure salvation for his own soul, and for the souls of his forefathers and descendents, Guillaume II, the ninth Lord of La Guerche, decided to found a collegiate church with twelve canons in 1206. In exchange for these "spiritual services" and the daily reciting of the office, he granted them a wide range of privileges.

Look for the excellent, and varied natural produce ; you can enjoy some of it on the spot.

VITRÉ

Standing on a spur of rock high above the R.Vilaine, Vitré Castle consists of a group of buildings, some of which date back to the 11th century, while others are 14th and 15th century. Towers, keeps, ramparts, machicolations, a drawbridge - it has all been meticulously restored and today it still looks impressive. It blends in perfectly with an urban environment that is itself very picturesque, with narrow streets and corbelled houses decorated with statues.

For many a long year, Vitré was famous for its weaving industry but it has now lost much of its former glory. Yet the town, with its population of 15,000, is still a bustling shopping centre, as well as an excellent place for a really good meal.

Vitré Castle.

CHATEAUBRIANT

This is the cradle of the Chateau-briand family whose name was originally written with a 'T' at the end. The first castle was built c.1000 A.D. by a lord named Brien. Much of this building is still standing and it now houses the sub-prefecture offices. The castle was partially restored in the 13th and 14th centuries. The other section, the so-called New Castle, dates only from the Renaissance.

The 13,000 people now living in the town faithfully keep alive the memory of the hostages who were shot on 22nd October 1941 by the forces occupying France.

ANCENIS

The present castle, now used as a school, has been subjected to a large number of restoration projects over the centuries but some parts of the building are still reminiscent of the old feudal fort. It saw the signing, on 14th September 1468, of one of the treaties that was to lead to the annexation of Brittany to France.

Ancenis stands on the right bank of the R.Loire. The other bank of the river belongs to the Anjou region and one of the nearby towns is none other than the famous **Liré** that was so dear to the poet Joachim du Bellay.

▲

Châteaubriant (Loire-Atlantique).

Le Grand-Fougeray (Ille-et-Vilaine) ▶

Kergournadec'h (Finistère)

CLISSON

For centuries, there was a large fortress in Clisson (which, in the year 1000 A.D. was written **Clizun**) but the castle, like the town, was destroyed during the Revolution by the Republican forces. The restoration work carried out during the Directorate and the Empire under the leadership of Senator Cacault has obviously altered the castle's original appearance. Nevertheless, there are many sections of the old fortress still in existence; they date back to the 13th, 14th and particularly the 15th centuries.

In the second courtyard of the area known as **The Manor**, visitors are shown a well which has now been filled in. During the Revolution, women, children and old people were thrown down it alive.

MACHECOUL

Machecoul's fortress, which was built at the same period as the one in Clisson, suffered the same fate during the French Revolution. And it did not have the good fortune to find a Senator Cacault to restore it. Because of this, all that remains today is a few stretches of wall overlooking the waters of the R.Falleson.

The most famous occupant of Machecoul Castle was undoubtedly one Gilles of Laval, companion to Joan of Arc, better known to criminal historians as Gilles of Retz, who was executed in Nantes on 26th October 1440.

THE COASTAL FORTRESSES

In addition to the **gateways to Brittany** lying on the marches of the Duchy, other fortresses were built on the shores of the ocean to prevent foreign invasion. This was the reason for the building of **Guérande, Belle-Ile** and **Quiberon, Port-Louis, Concarneau, Camaret, Brest, Château du Taureau** (Bull Castle) at the mouth of the R.Morlaix, the **Fort de la Latte** at Cape Fréhel, and finally the citadel in **Saint-Malo** that wrought havoc over the centuries during every attempt by English troops to set foot on French soil by means of landings on the peninsula.

But Brittany has one other stronghold which has resisted many an attack over the course of the centuries...

Port-Louis (Morbihan). ▶

The ramparts of the old walled town in Concarneau. ▼

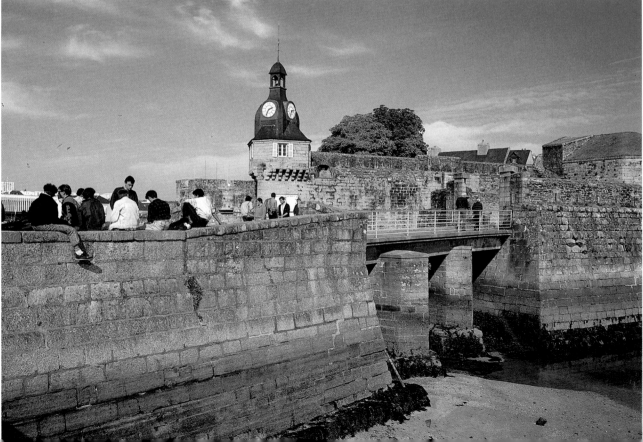

Fort-la-Latte Castle

THE BRETON LANGUAGE

Nearly one million people still speak Breton. It is one of the Celtic languages, closely-related to Welsh and, to a lesser degree, to the various Gaelic dialects spoken in Scotland and Ireland.

From the 10th century onwards, the geographical limit of the Breton language has always been to the west of a line joining Plouha on the northern coast to the mouth of the R. Vilaine or even, at the turn of the century, as far as the Guérande region on the south coast. Yet in the eastern part of the peninsula, place-names show that Breton was spoken for several hundred years.

In a region where the oral tradition has almost always been more important than written texts, literary output in Breton was limited until recently (let's say until the 18th and 19th centuries) to the popular ballads, songs, and love songs that constitute the **gwerziou** and the **soniou**. Today, though, well-established writers and poets use the Celtic language with great success. This is so for J.P. Calloc'h, Jakez Riou, Tanguy Malmanche, Youenn Drézen, and Xavier de Langlais, just as it is the case for Angéla Duval, Youenn Gwernig, and Pierre-Jakez Hélias, the author of **Horse of Pride**, not forgetting a number of singers such as Alan Stivel and Gilles Servat.

There is ample proof of the loyalty shown by the Bretons to the **old language of their ancestors**, even if they do not speak it themselves. Just look at the names people give their houses or their boats.

One example among thousands of others is the name of **Pen-Duik** that Eric Tabarly chose for his yachts. **Pen-Duik** means **Little Black Head**, the Breton for "titmouse". But in this case, the titmouse is a wonderful sea bird !

Vauban's fortress on Belle-Ile. ▶

La Motte-Tanguy Castle and Tower in Brest.

The start of a great adventure.

A long-distance runner : a trimaran. ▶

DEEP-SEA AND INSHORE FISHING

The Bretons living along the coast look out on the infinity of the ocean and have always drawn much of their living from fishing. In the Middle Ages, cod could still be found in Breton waters. Gradually, the Bretons became accustomed to following the fish wherever it sought refuge, in Scandinavian waters, near Newfoundland, off Iceland and, these days, in the Barents Sea. For centuries, Paimpol and the neighbouring ports were the capital of cod fishing and its tragedies provided the inspiration for Pierre Loti's book, **Iceland Fisherman**.

Nowadays, only the fleets from Saint-Malo and Cancale still go northwards **deep sea fishing**. But strong trawlers equipped with deep freezes have replaced the legendary schooners sailed by Breton crews until the 1930's.

In addition to the deep-sea fishing industry, the passing years have seen the development of an inshore fishing industry specialising in the fish and shellfish that are commonest close to the shores of the peninsula - sardines, mackerel, conger eels, skate, lobster, spiny lobster, and crab. Some of them are fished on lines, others trawled. Shellfish are caught in baskets.

Harvests from the sea.

Quiberon Harbour.

The strand at Saint-Père Harbour near Saint-Malo. ▲

Dahouët Harbour ▶

A number of small ports still have individual boats but, over the last fifty years, a veritable fishing industry has grown up in Lorient and Concarneau, as well as in Douarnenez and Camaret. This brought modern trawlers on to the scene, the factory ships, deep-freeze clippers, and great lobster boats that travel further and further afield to catch the precious food provided by the ocean.

THE BANKS

The trawlers operate mainly on the **Banks**, in the waters stretching from the furthermost headlands of Brittany and the capes of Ireland or further west up to 240 nautical miles from Ushant.

The area consists of a huge submerged base with underwater valleys called **beds**, separated by mountain ranges, and all the features run in a north-east to south-west direction. It is the peaks of the uplands that form the banks. Their names crop up frequently in conversation on the jetties in Lorient or Concarneau - **Great Sole, Banc Germain, Cockburn, Banc Labadie, Little Sole, Melville Bank, Jones Bank, Shamrock, Parson Bank, Banc de la Chapelle** etc.

The tunny and spiny lobster fishermen travel even greater distances.

Lobster-boats coming back to port.

◄*Concarneau Harbour.*

They are often to be found off the African coasts (Banc d'Arguin or Gulf of Guinea) or in the waters of the Caribbean where the presence of "intruders" is not always appreciated by the locals.

For visitors, the landing of the catches on the quayside in Lorient, Concarneau or Douarnenez, is a unique sight. So is the auction sale. Yet here, as elsewhere, it is a privilege only enjoyed by early birds. The best time of the day during summer is 5 a.m. !

All the fish and shellfish find their way onto the best tables in France, including the ones along the Mediterranean where the so-called "local" red mullet, like the famous bass cooked with fennel, are delivered directly by the fish traders of Brittany.

The remainder of the catches are taken to canning factories to be turned into sardines in oil, mackerel in white wine, Concarneau-style tuna fish, or frozen fillets of fish. The **Brittany** label is a sure sign of quality for consumers.

CHAPELS, CHURCHES, WAYSIDE CROSSES AND FOUNTAINS

Brittany has always been a region rich in vernacular architecture and art. Very few areas provide such large numbers and such a wide variety of elaborate buildings showing both the creativity and the religious fervour of a people that found their expression whenever historical circumstances permitted.

Although there are very few traces of the earliest Romanesque buildings, the Gothic period has left a multitude of chapels, churches and even cathedrals. Almost everywhere the towers, particularly the finely traceried belltowers, are a source of wonder to visitors. Among the most elegant are the Kreisker in Saint-Pol-de-Léon, and le Folgoët (both 15th century) not forgetting the one in Pleyben (16th century).

The churches and chapels house marvellous roodscreens, altar screens, baptisteries, and pulpits, all of them wonderfully carved. They date from the 12th, 14th and 15th centuries. Some of the stained glass windows also date back to these periods, like the ones in the cathedrals in Dol, Tréguier, la Roche-Derrien and Saint-Fiacre near Le Faouët. Some of the chapels still have coloured frescoes, in varying states of repair, the best-known being in Kernascldéen (15th century).

The chapel in Le Vieux-Bourg de Plé-hérel (Côtes-du-Nord).

St. John's Chapel on the banks of the R. Elorn (Finistère).

Notre-Dame de Tronoën (Finistère).

Notre-Dame du Port-Blanc

Quimper : the Rue Kéréon and the cathedral.

Tréguier Cathedral : the nave. ▶

A fountain in Briec near Quimper.

◄ *Saint-Thégonnec (Finistère).*

In addition, there are the porches and, inside the buildings, thousands of old statues, most of them representing the bishops and saints that people Brittany's legends.

More impressive are the **calvaries** or wayside crosses, with stone carvings representing scenes from Christ's Passion. Most of them were erected in the 15th century or more especially in the latter years of the following century after the plague epidemic that had ravaged the whole of Europe. The Finistère with Tronoën, Guimiliau, Plougastel-Daoulas, Pleyben, Saint-Vénec, and Quinilen, the Côtes-du-Nord with Lanrivain, and the Morbihan with Guéhenno are privileged to have the finest of all the wayside crosses. Visitors always enjoy counting the number of statues carved by the old craftsmen - there are over one hundred on some, one hundred and fifty or even two hundred on others, some on foot, others on horseback, all of them wearing mediaeval or Renaissance costume. A marvellous sight for anybody who is keen on popular art.

In addition to the churches, chapels, and calvaries, there are the sacred springs sheltered beneath a small stone monument. They may bear witness to a particular cult that preceded the Christian era but which was later taken over by Christianity. Unless (this is another hypothesis) the cult was a later implantation brought by the immigrants from across the Channel.

The wayside cross in Guimiliau.

Notre-Dame de la Joie (Our Lady of Joy, Finistère). ▶

◀*The wayside cross in Plougastel-Daoulas.*

A cross near the chapel in Le Croaziou between Pont-l'Abbé and Loctudy.

Guimiliau : the interior of the church.

Daoulas : the Romanesque-style cloisters. ▶

◀Le Faouët : a roodscreen in St. Fiacre's Chapel.

Loc-Envel (Côtes-du-Nord) : hanging keystone representing Christ and God the Father.

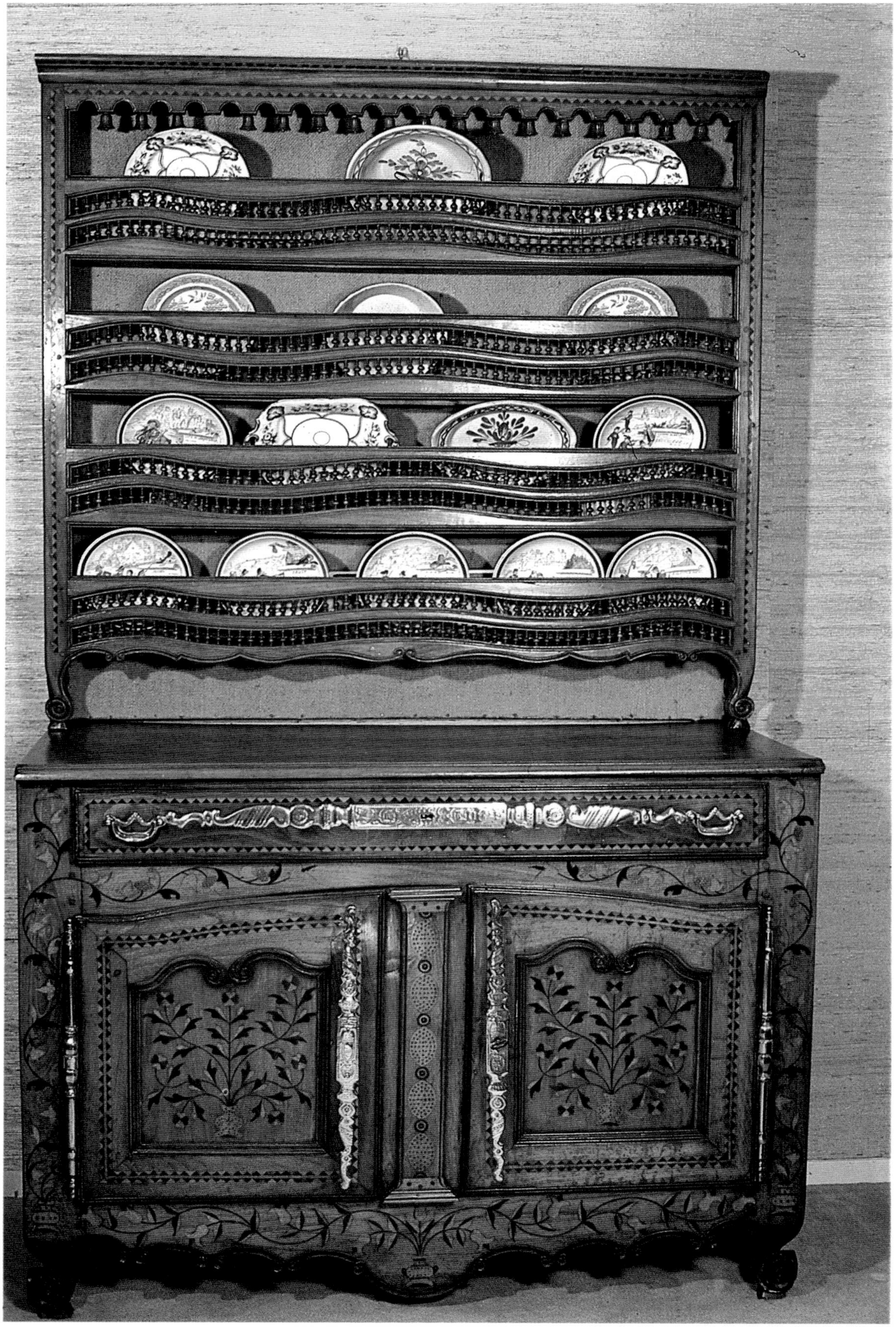

19th-century cradle made by V. Brantôme and Le Blaye.

◄ *A dresser (private collection).*

A chest.

BRETON FURNITURE

The creativity of the Bretons, who built church towers and carved wayside crosses, is again evident when it comes to furniture. Craftsmen abound and, over the centuries, they have lovingly made the great closets, box-beds, chests, dressers and sideboards that are still visible in many a home where families have preferred not to replace them by the results of mass production.

There are a number of museums that have large areas devoted to Breton furniture with its marquetry and gold-headed nails. The museum in Rennes is outstanding in this respect.

The "Odetta" earthenware made at the turn of the century. Quimper Faïence Museum.

"The reed-gatherers", an oval earthenware platter. Quimper Faïence Museum.

POTTERY, EARTHENWARE AND CRAFTS

In many places, especially in the villages of Argoat, there are still a number of potters who are striving against all the odds to maintain the traditional craft of the Breton potters of days long gone.

Breton earthenware factories are better known. Most of them are in Quimper but there are others that are just as highly thought of. If you're interested in this subject, make sure you avoid buying certain products

that are of really mediocre quality. The mere fact that they have a label showing their origin cannot hide the fact that the manufacturers had purely commercial interests at heart.

It's easier to choose some of the fine lace in the Bigouden area or some of the magnificent hand-woven materials which also maintain an age-old tradition from the days when Brittany exported its products throughout Europe and even as far

away as the Spanish colonies in Latin America.

It takes only a few prestigious pieces of faïence, or glazed earthenware, from the best workshops in the Cornouaille area placed on a polished oak table covered with a Locronan tablecloth to bring to life the truth that was so well expressed by Paul Féval :

"A meal is always the most important part of Breton hospitality."

123

BRITTANY'S COOKING AND FOOD

So what do we eat in Brittany? What traditional dishes will you find in this vast region stretching over five départements (counties)?

Right along the coast, you will be able to enjoy shellfish, crustaceans, and the innumerable varieties of fresh fish landed every day by the pinnaces and trawlers.

Top of the list, of course, come the oysters that are so carefully cultivated in special oyster parks in Cancale, the R.Morlaix, and the inlets, as well as in the estuary of the R.Belon and all along the coast between the Morbihan Gulf and the mouth of the R.Vilaine. These are the famous European oysters, usually known as **Belons**.

In addition to the world-renowned oysters, there are mussels, clams, and scallops. And as for crustaceans, there are lobsters, spiny lobsters, scampi, various types of crab, and shrimps.

That should be sufficient to make a pleasant start to any meal. Next comes the fish course, with a whole range of varieties and just as many ways of preparing it. On the south coast, the "cotriades" or fish stews are a must, and they are a meal in themselves. During the summer, though, sardines reign supreme along a large stretch of coastline.

In the Argoat, or inland Brittany, river fish like trout and salmon have pride of place. And there is a wide range of pork-based products -

pâtés, roast back, chitterlings large and small, sausages and black puddings.

As far as meat is concerned, local lamb is one of the best in Europe, especially when it comes from the salt marshes. Like the veal, beef and poultry, it is garnished with top-quality vegetables, such as the early spring vegetables (potatoes, carrots, cabbages, cauliflowers, onions and beans) picked both inland and on the coast.

The Nantes area offers gourmets a very high-class cuisine, the outstanding dishes being fish from the R.Loire (with the famous white butter sauce that often accompanies them), poultry (with a special mention for Nantes duckling), and a multitude of other produce. All of them can be pleasantly washed down with the excellent local dry white wines (Muscadet and Gros-Plant), red wines (Gamay from the Loire area) and rosés (Groslot de Retz).

Wherever you are, you cannot fail to appreciate the incomparable taste of Brittany's butter, which has been famous throughout Europe since the Middle Ages. Not to mention the buckwheat savoury pancakes, the dessert pancakes made with wheat flour, and the cakes, all of them accompanied by sparkling cider.

In all, seen from this angle as from many others, Brittany is a region where people get a lot out of life.

Breton fare : seafood platter, ''far'', Breton lardy cake (kuign-aman) and pancakes.

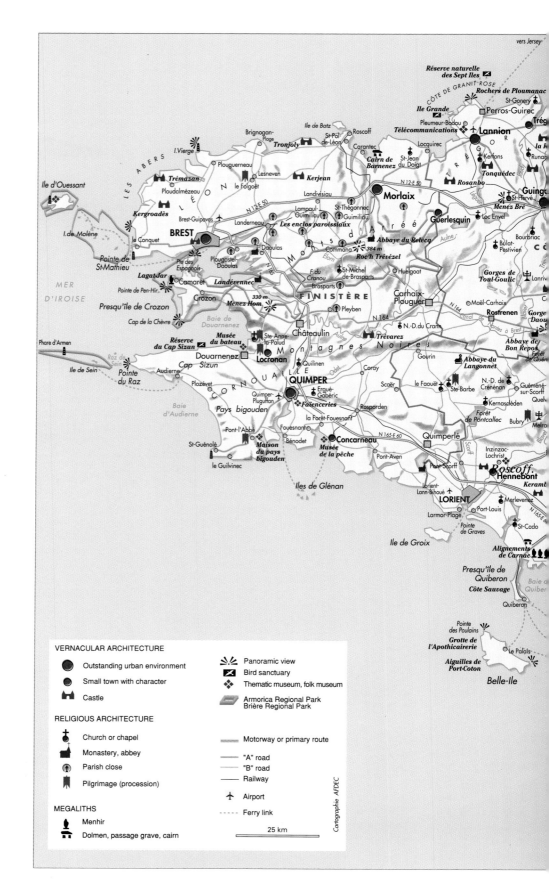

Saint-Pol-de-Léon.

VERNACULAR ARCHITECTURE

- ⬤ Outstanding urban environment
- ● Small town with character
- 🏰 Castle

RELIGIOUS ARCHITECTURE

- ☩ Church or chapel
- ⛪ Monastery, abbey
- ⛪ Parish close
- ▮ Pilgrimage (procession)

MEGALITHS

- ⚲ Menhir
- ⛩ Dolmen, passage grave, cairn

- ⚡ Panoramic view
- ◀ Bird sanctuary
- ❖ Thematic museum, folk museum
- ▱ Armorica Regional Park
  Brière Regional Park

- ═══ Motorway or primary route
- ──── "A" road
- ──── "B" road
- ──── Railway
- ✈ Airport
- - - - Ferry link

25 km

Cartographie AFDEC

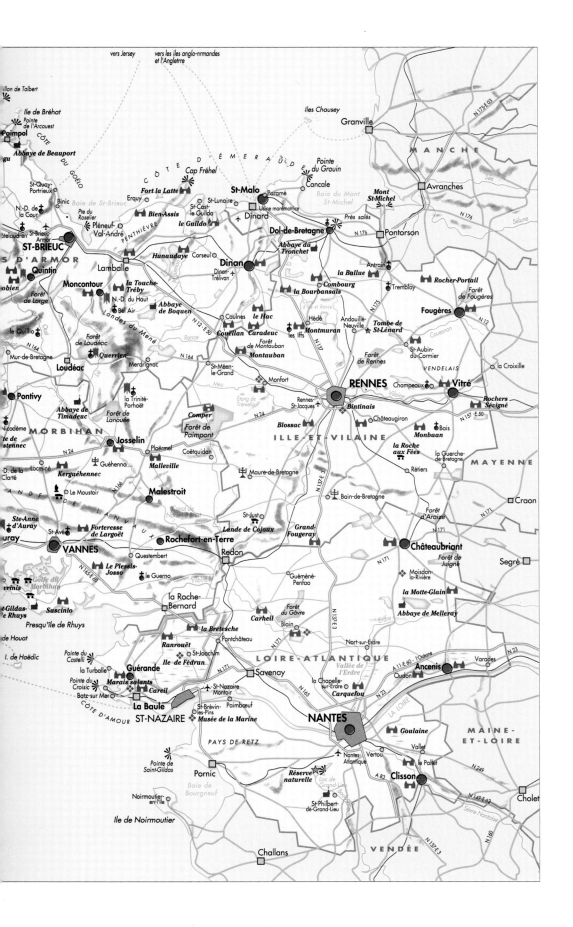

TABLE OF CONTENTS

Introduction 3

Map 4

Map 5

The end of the world 10

The highlands of Brittany 14

A mild healthy climate 16

Armorica's soul 18

Breathe in the ozone 20

The Argoat and Armor 21

Armorica and the Armoricans 24

Minos, Cadiz and the Morbihan 27

Brittany of the standing stones. 30

The grandeur and decline of the Celts of Armorica. 33

The arrival of the Bretons 39

Plou, Ker and Tre in abundance 42

The Brittany of the saints 45

The Bretons enter the history books 50

Four centuries of war. 52

Blois v. Montfort or the War of Breton Sucession 60

The "Insane War" : Saint-Aubin-du-Cormier 61

Duchess and Queen. 71

4th August 1532 : the Act of Union 72

The League, revolts and conspiracies 73

Celts to the fore 76

Chateaubriand and the Romantic Revival 80

The Breton character 81

Making real contact 85

The coastal fortresses 91

The Breton language 92

Deep-sea and inshore fishing.. 98

From the Banks to the Caribbean 100

Chapels, churches, wayside crosses and fountains 104

Breton furniture 121

Pottery, earthenware and crafts 123

Brittany's food and cooking 125

PHOTOGRAPHIC CREDITS

H. Boulé : front cover, p. 6, 21, 30, 34-35, 36, 37, 38, 44, 45, 46, 47, 49, 57, 59, 91b., 93, 94-95, 100, 101b, 105, 106b, 109, 110, 118, 124, 87 and back cover. **J.-L. Barbelette** : p. 84. **H. Champollion** : p. 3, 8, 9, 12-13, 15, 16, 17, 20, 22-23, 25, 31, 33, 48, 51, 53, 61, 63, 65, 67, 78, 81, 86, 88, 90, 92, 101h., 103, 108, 112, 115, 116-117, 119. **L.-C. Duchesne** : p. 41, 43, 107. **G. Daniel** : p. 40, 58. **J. Duval** : p. 83. **N. Fediaevsky** : p. 24, 28-29, 32, 39, 54, 56, 62 h., 64, 68, 69, 71, 73, 74, 75, 99, 102, 122, 123. **A. Fouquet** : p. 2 m., 27, 42. **J.-P. Gisserot** : p. 2 h. and b., 50, 60, 62b., 79, 82, 89, 111, 114. **N. Guiriec** : p. 26. **C. Jacq** : p. 106 h. **J. Le Berd** : p. 91 h. **M. Ogier** : p. 120, 121. **J.-C. Phillipot** : p. 80. **J.-P. Prével** : p. 7, 66, 76, 96, 97. **J.-Y. Ruaux** : p. 70. **P. Sigard** : p. 90. **M. Thersiquel** : p. 11, 18, 19. **P. Thomas** : p. 72.

Cet ouvrage a été imprimé par Mame Imprimeurs à Tours (37)

I.S.B.N. 2.7373.0144.0 - Dépôt légal : mars 1988 - N° éditeur : 1465.04.03.04.93